Colors

Brown
Seeing Brown All around Us

by Michael Dahl

Consulting Editor: Gail Saunders-Smith, PhD

Capstone
press

Mankato, Minnesota

A+ Books are published by Capstone Press,
151 Good Counsel Drive, P.O. Box 669, Mankato, Minnesota 56002.
www.capstonepress.com

1 2 3 4 5 6 10 09 08 07 06 05

Library of Congress Cataloging-in-Publication Data
Dahl, Michael.
    Brown: seeing brown all around us / by Michael Dahl.
    p. cm.—(A+ Books. Colors)
    Includes bibliographical references and index.
    ISBN 0-7368-3669-1 (hardcover)
    ISBN 0-7368-5071-6 (paperback)
    1. Brown—Juvenile literature. 2. Color—Juvenile literature. I. Title. II. Series.
QC495.5.D344 2005
535.6—dc22   2004014678

Summary: Text and photographs describe common things that are brown, including grocery bags, footballs, and teddy bears.

Credits

Blake A. Hoena, editor; Heather Kindseth, designer; Kelly Garvin, photo researcher

Photo Credits

All images provided by Capstone Press/Gary Sundermeyer, except for Capstone Press/Karon Dubke, 14–15, 32 (dog)

Note to Parents, Teachers, and Librarians
The Colors books use full-color photographs and a nonfiction format to introduce children to the world of color. *Brown* is designed to be read aloud to a pre-reader or to be read independently by an early reader. Photographs and activities help listeners and early readers understand the text and concepts discussed. The book encourages further learning by including the following sections: Table of Contents, Glossary, Read More, Internet Sites, and Index. Early readers may need assistance using these features.

Table of Contents

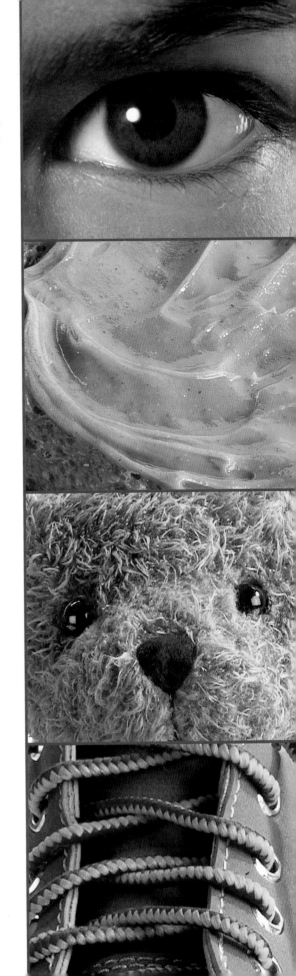

Brown can lift you off the floor.

Grocery bags are made to be easy to use. They pop open with a flick of the wrist. Their square bottoms make them stand upright as they are being filled.

Brown holds groceries from the store.

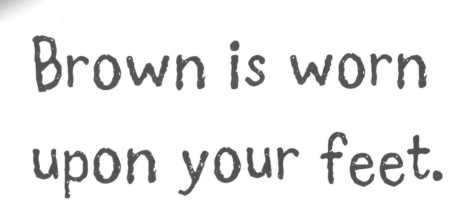

Thousands and thousands of years ago, people didn't have shoes or boots. They tied folded-up grass leaves to their feet.

Brown is worn upon your feet.

Brownies are not just a kind of treat. Girl Scouts between the ages of 6 and 8 are called Brownies.

Brown is sweet and fun to eat.

It takes about 550 peanuts to make a 12-ounce jar of peanut butter.

Brown is creamy.
Brown is thick.

Dogs can learn to do tricks, such as sit, fetch, and roll over. What tricks does your dog know how to do?

Brown can learn to do a trick.

Brown gets kicked.
Brown gets passed.

One nickname for a football is "pigskin." But footballs aren't made out of pig skins. They are made out of cow leather.

Chocolate is the second most popular flavor of ice cream. Vanilla is the first.

Brown is sweet and melting fast.

Brown can blink.
Brown can stare.

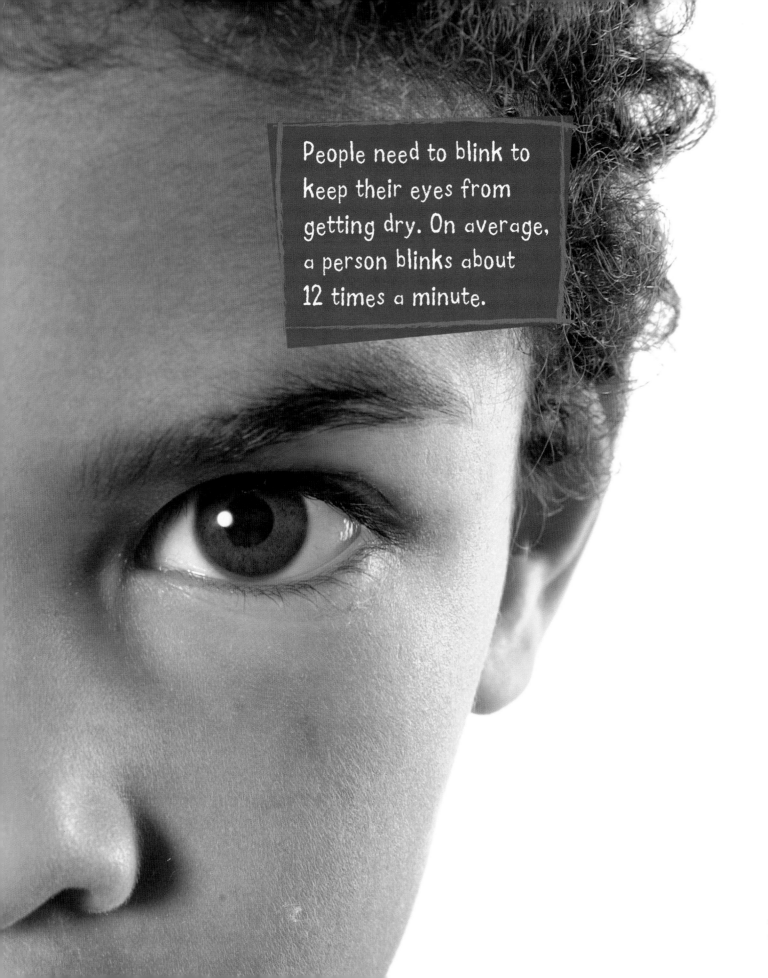

People need to blink to keep their eyes from getting dry. On average, a person blinks about 12 times a minute.

Tree bark is like a person's skin. Bark protects a tree's insides. It also expands as the tree grows.

Brown grows branches in the air.

Brown can warm you when you're cold.

About 3,000 years ago, people in South America drank the first hot chocolate. They added ground-up cacao beans to hot water to make a chocolate-flavored drink.

Brown is fun
to hug and hold.

Peanut Butter Clay

Artists work with different kinds of materials to create art. They even use food. You can make clay out of peanut butter.

You will need

1 cup (240 mL) creamy peanut butter

½ cup (120 mL) honey

2 cups (480 mL) nonfat powdered milk

dry-ingredient measuring cups

medium bowl

mixing spoon

1 Pour peanut butter and honey into the bowl and mix.

2 Add 1 cup (240 mL) powdered milk to the bowl and mix. Then slowly add small amounts of the remaining powdered milk. Continue mixing and adding powdered milk until the clay is no longer sticky. Don't add too much, or the clay will be crumbly.

3 Use the clay to make shapes and animals.

Glossary

blink (BLINGK)—to move your eyelids down and up very quickly

branch (BRANCH)—a part of a tree that grows out of its trunk like an arm

cacao bean (kuh-KOU BEEN)—the seed of the cacao tree; cacao beans are used to make chocolate.

expand (ek-SPAND)—to grow larger

fetch (FECH)—to go after and bring back something or somebody

groceries (GROH-sur-eez)—the food people buy from a store

leather (LETH-ur)—animal skin used to make shoes, bags, and other goods

protect (pruh-TEKT)—to keep safe

vanilla (vuh-NIL-uh)—a type of flavoring used in foods, such as ice cream, cookies, and candy

Read More

Eck, Kristin. *Colors in My House.* Look-and-Learn Books. New York: PowerKids Press, 2004.

Mitchell, Melanie. *Brown.* First Step Nonfiction. Minneapolis: Lerner, 2004.

Whitehouse, Patricia. *Brown Foods.* The Colors We Eat. Chicago: Heinemann, 2004.

Internet Sites

FactHound offers a safe, fun way to find Internet sites related to this book. All of the sites on FactHound have been researched by our staff.

Here's how:
1. Visit *www.facthound.com*
2. Type in this special code 0736836691 for age-appropriate sites. Or enter a search word related to this book for a more general search.
3. Click on the Fetch It button.

FactHound will fetch the best sites for you!

Index